Up From The Ashes

A Healing Journey through Sexual Trauma, Domestic Violence and Addictions

Kathy Morris

Balboa Press books may be ordered through booksellers or by contacting:

Balboa Press
A Division of Hay House
1663 Liberty Drive
Bloomington, IN 47403
www.balboapress.com
1 (877) 407-4847

Print information available on the last page.

ISBN: 978-1-5043-7234-3 (sc)
ISBN: 978-1-5043-7233-6 (e)

Library of Congress Control Number: 2016921536

Balboa Press rev. date: 02/06/2017

Contents

Message to the Reader

It is important to deal with your emotional and spiritual health. Just as you would go to the doctor with a broken leg or pain anywhere in your body, it is equally important to pay attention to the hole in your soul. By healing, I discovered my soul's true purpose.

My message to you is that you should not be afraid to face your fears because they will teach you what you need to know. Allow forgiveness and unconditional love to guide your path. I had blind faith in my therapist, who would say I've changed. But I always felt the same—miserable, insecure, dirty, and unworthy of life. I learned when you are abused at a young age, you must work harder at everything. My history has made me the person I am today, and because of the abuse, I have been able to allow spirit to speak through me and use me as a vessel. I forgave both parents. When my journey started, I was not able to bless my past, but today I am a powerful woman who has risen from the ashes. I now walk a spiritual path and am appreciative of my gifts. I wake up every day in gratitude, allowing love to guide my every step.

My message to you is that you can overcome your adversities. When I began my healing journey, I asked, "Show me someone who has healed from incest." I continued my search for such a person until one day I looked up and realized it was me. Now I am teaching others how to heal. –Kathy Morris

Foreword

I am honored and grateful to have had the opportunity to work with Kathy during the past eight years as client and business partner. Her unique ability to share, heal and teach transformed my life. While working with her, new lessons were learned from her powerful story.

As I read Up From the Ashes, my emotions changed from sadness with each painful chapter to hope with her eventual successful healing and triumph. The pain of an innocent child suffering abuse and neglect was seared in my brain. It was only because I was sitting across from a powerful and compassionate woman, that I could continue reading. I knew she had not only survived but was thriving. She is a living example of unconditional love and forgiveness. Up from the Ashes is the true story of Kathy's ability to heal from unspeakable trauma and share the lessons learned with others. After reading Up from the Ashes, you will have a new understanding of your capacity to heal, overcome, and transform.

-Sheila Quarles
Business Partner & Friend

Prologue

One unseasonably warm day in early March 1986, after being on the Philadelphia police force for twelve years, I went to work just as I always did. That day, my career changed in the blink of an eye.

We were given orders from the sergeant at roll call to disperse gamblers on the corner. While patrolling, I spotted a group of males gambling at the corner of Twelfth and Market. I drove past, pretending not to see them, and parked my patrol car one block away at Thirteenth and Market. I got out of my car to walk toward the gamblers. Halfway down the twelve hundred block of Market, one of the male gamblers was walking toward me. When he saw me, he darted out into the oncoming traffic. I stepped off the curb, anxiously waiting for the flow of traffic to pass, keeping my eyes on him running down the subway stairs across the street. With my adrenalin pumping and while looking left toward the traffic, a car parked on my right backed up, hitting and throwing me into oncoming traffic. I fell down, feeling as though I was moving in slow motion, with my gun going in one direction and my night stick falling in another. I twisted my left leg and clenched my teeth as I went down.

I lay in the middle of the street looking up at the sky, not noticing the bus that stopped just short of hitting me. Everything went silent around me and stopped. I looked up, and the sergeant slowly came into focus. He called for transportation. The ambulance arrived, and I was transported to the hospital. I was at the hospital for four hours. Everything seemed to hurt.

I was released from the hospital with a cane. I thought I would return to work in a few weeks. Several months later I was still in pain and on disability leave.

After a knee operation and twenty-four months of physical therapy, I was placed on permanent disability. I went from working rotating shifts six days a week to now staring at the ceiling, thinking about my future. I had no idea what I wanted to do with my life. I felt relieved and scared. I knew for a long time I was not operating at my full potential. I wanted to make a change, but fear prevailed and kept me feeling stuck. Now I had been given the gift of time. This inner journey of self-discovery unearthed many secrets, which ultimately led to my personal growth. I reviewed my life choices and realized I needed to face many internal demons.

Chapter 1

Childhood Memories

My earliest feelings about my mother were always those of fear and being abandoned. I never felt connected to her. I remember her putting me outside on the sidewalk in front of our row home. As I looked through the wooden bars of my playpen, it seems as though I was very close to the ground. Everything felt as though it towered over me. I felt small, vulnerable, and overwhelmed by helplessness, with no family members outside and me on a tiny street in North Philadelphia. Even though it was warm and sunny, I felt sad, alone, and afraid. I could see adults walking up and down the street. They seemed close, but they were out of reach. One woman walked past me every day. When I got older, I realized she was our neighbor, Mrs. Walker. Somehow I connected with her. I smiled as she walked by and waved. She walked with a limp, almost on her ankles, because of her bad feet. She was coming home from her job at the local factory. The memory of her reminded me of how much I was ignored by my own mother.

When I was five years old, my father and mother were arguing one Sunday morning because he had come home drunk the night before. My sisters and I were sitting at the kitchen table, eating breakfast, when my mother suddenly jumped up from her seat, grabbed the iron, took the cord, and wrapped it around his neck. She was trying her best to strangle him right before our eyes. I left my body, and I don't remember what happened next. I was scared and helpless and thought I was next, so I withdrew into my mind and became very quiet. I was careful not to be noticed. The only person I talked to was my sister, Val, who was three years older.

As far back as I can remember, I felt afraid in my parents' house. My mother was full of rage, screaming from the top of her lungs when my father came home drunk every weekend. Sometimes on Monday morning, as I was heading out to school, I would find my father sleeping in the vestibule floor. I quietly stepped over him and continued on to school. The house was always chaotic. I worked hard at staying away from my mother, but she was upset most of the time, which usually resulted in her directing her rage at me by yelling and lobbing constant criticism in my direction.

I constantly lived in my mind and daydreamed about when I would escape the madness. I began very slowly to build a deep-seated hatred for myself. I never felt comfortable in my body and felt there was something profoundly wrong with me. My mother told me every day, "You will never amount to anything, and you are just like your no-good, drunken father." This message was implanted in my brain. I thought it must be true.

Daddy disappeared every weekend. He left for work Thursday morning and did not return until Sunday night. I always worried he would not come back. When he did return, I felt relieved, but all hell would break loose. The fights would start, and I thought, *This is my fault.* My mother would run after my father, screaming, "motherfucker," "shit," and a lot of other words I knew were bad. I would go into my room, pull the covers over my head, and cry quietly to myself.

One day when I was five, my mother dressed me in new

clothes and patent-leather shoes. She took my hand, and we walked for about twenty minutes. When we arrived at a strange building, she let go of my hand and left. I thought she had decided to leave me and never come back. There was no explanation of why I was there. She didn't sit down and tell me I was going to go to school and that this was kindergarten.

There were other small children playing outside, but all I could think of was that I had been left in the back of this big building. When we were told to come inside, there were cookies and warm milk, nap time, and playtime with drawing, coloring, and cut-outs, none of which I was interested in. I could not relax because I was distraught, thinking about never seeing my family again. My mind raced with the fear. I sat there all day lifeless, unhappy, and unsure. I had no idea what would happen to me. Kindergarten was traumatic. I thought my mother had abandoned me. I wanted to leave, but I didn't remember how to get home. Finally, at the end of the day, I saw a familiar face. Val was waiting for me outside, and all my fears slowly disappeared. It was Val's job to pick me up after school. She held my hand and walked me home. She was my saving grace, and I held on tightly. I never forgot the fear of that first day of school.

Sometime during my kindergarten year, I had my tonsils removed. Once again, my mother did not explain that I would be staying overnight in the hospital. I was left in an unfamiliar place, thinking that they were not coming back for me. At the hospital, I hid under the bed, afraid. The nurses never understood why I was always hiding. After two days, my mother came to take me home. She was mad and not happy to see me. She hailed a cab because I was still woozy from the anesthesia. She never said a word to me. When I got home, Val helped me climb the steps and remove my clothes so I could get in bed. I thought I was dying because my throat was in such extreme pain. Val brought me soup and then ice cream. She sat and talked to me. I don't remember seeing my mother the rest of the night. I was happy Val was there.

At age six, I was in the first grade and did not know how to groom my hair. My mother was sleeping, and I needed her to comb my hair. I slowly walked down the hall to her bedroom door and took a deep breath before I knocked. My mother considered her bedroom sacred ground; we were never allowed in.

I was afraid to wake her up, so I slowly opened the door and quietly asked, "Mom, can you please help me with my hair?"

She jumped up and screamed, "Get the hell out of my room, and never bother me when I am sleeping."

I was paralyzed with fear. It took a moment for me to recover from the assault. I turned around and went back to my room, tears streaming down my face. I tried to do something with my hair. I went to school unkempt and depressed.

My first-grade teacher realized I was having a hard time hearing. She moved my seat from the rear of the room to the front, and my grades improved. I also developed a speech impediment. The teacher sent a note home to my mother, explaining my symptoms. I was given a speech therapist at school, and my mother took me to see the ear, nose, and throat (ENT) doctor. We caught the bus together to get to the doctor's office. I was not excited about spending one-on-one time with my mother. She was cold and distant and seemed angry every time I was alone with her. We never spoke during the bus ride. I was examined by the ENT doctor, and it was determined I needed an operation on my ears. My mother seemed agitated with the news from the doctor. Returning on the bus, we rode for a short time, and suddenly, she got off, leaving me without any explanation. I was afraid. I rode for what seemed like an eternity before the bus driver tried to get my attention. I was staring out the window, so he got up from the driver's seat, grabbed my hands, and helped me exit. I was petrified as I stood on the sidewalk, looking around, trying to figure out which way to go to school. I was lost. I walked in the wrong direction for one block and then turned around and walked back. I kept ending up right back where I originally got off the bus. This happened over and over again until I frantically decided to run across the street with tears in my eyes. Once I was across the street, things looked familiar, and I started walking. Three blocks later, I reached my elementary school, Pratt Arnold, at Twenty-Second and Susquehanna Streets.

Three weeks later, my mother took me to the hospital. I did not know I was scheduled for an operation. Tubes were placed in my ears to drain fluid and wax from them. When I returned home, Val took care of me again, bringing food and water and sitting and talking with me. My mother totally rejected me. She never came to check on me. Val was my caregiver. As a result of my mother's actions, I was in a constant state of fear. I felt that I was unwanted and that something was wrong with me. I began to blame myself for how I was treated

My mother gave me many household chores. I ironed my father's handkerchiefs, underwear, and sheets. I was responsible for his clothes as well as my own. Val and I could not reach the sink, so we stood on chairs to wash the dishes. I had to scrub floors on my hands and knees. I hated housework. The only kind of contact my mother had with me was negative and painful. She was often angry; she criticized and berated me. I could never do anything to please her.

My mother wore beautiful, elegant clothes that were hand-sewn and designed for her by a seamstress. She was a very proud, beautiful woman. Her outside persona was highly revered by family and community. She belonged to an elite social club that traveled to different cities. I remember my father taking us to the airport. As we watched her plane take off from the airport's large window, I had the sinking feeling she might not come home.

She was a socialite who kept company with many local celebrities. This was a stark difference from the person I knew at home

I would escape the chaos by playing with Val. We played cards on the weekend into the wee hours of the morning. We were told to turn the lights out and go to bed. We did, but we'd put covers over our heads, turn on our flashlights, and play until we both became so sleepy that we felt dizzy. These were times I felt free and childlike.

My father took me to the Uptown Theater to a live X-rated entertainer when I was seven. The show was at night, starring Mom's Mabley. It was my first time seeing a live show. I was thrilled. I remember being dressed up in my white Sunday dress. When I got inside, I sat in the seat beside my father. I was so small that my feet did not touch the floor. Even though I didn't understand what was being said, I loved being with my father and the excitement of live entertainment. Mom's Mabley was known for using profanity and sexual explicit jokes. I didn't realize until I was an adult, how inappropriate it was for me to be there. I was the only child in the theatre. The following year, at age eight, I would walk a mile from my home to attend the Saturday matinee shows alone. I saw all of the Motown acts, James Brown, Stevie Wonder, Temptations, The Four Tops, and many more.

When I was nine, my father pitted me against my mother. He told me intimate details of their relationship. He would secretly tell me that they weren't having sex and that she was treating him badly. I remember him saying that "a man needed sex." Often, while he was talking to me, my mother would go off into a rage and blame me for listening to him. This was confusing. I wanted to disappear. I felt my mother despised me.

I hated the approach of the holidays. The tension in the house would escalate. My mother would get into a cleaning frenzy, cleaning every crevice of the house. All of her relatives would come to the house for dinner. Everything—and I mean every single thing—had to be perfect. We'd scrub down of the entire house. Every dish, every cabinet in the house had to be cleaned, and everything inside the cabinets had to be washed and cleaned. Every piece of wood furniture had to be waxed and polished to a shine.

There was a time when my mother wanted the living and dining rooms freshly painted for the holidays, which meant that the wallpaper had to be removed. I remember that we began that project two weeks before Christmas Day. We were up all night scraping wallpaper. My sister, my mother, my father, and I were scraping wallpaper from the walls. It was not fun. My father decided to leave the house in the middle of the project. When he didn't come right back, my mother screamed at my sister and me, transferring her anger from him to us. I hated the daily tension and chaos. It always intensified with each approaching holiday.

It was an Easter tradition for the family to go to church. On one particular Easter, my father went out on Saturday night and did not get home until early Sunday morning. While everyone was asleep, he stumbled around in the dining room and mistakenly thought he was urinating in the bathroom. He urinated and vomited on our Easter hats. My mother was furious. These were our special Easter bonnets. We could not go to church without a hat, so she cleaned the hats to the best of her ability, and insisted that we wear them. We all went to church in silence. It was important to her to maintain the family image. Val and I sat in church with our urine and putrid-smelling hats, while my father reeked of alcohol and my mother sat with her rage.

After church we went to Aunt Annie's house to have dinner. Alcohol was a big part of family holidays and celebrations. I think this was a contributing factor to most of the family chaos. As soon as we entered, the drinking and dancing started. I had fun watching my parents and relatives socialize. It was like a show. My father would dance close to other women, and my mother would get angry. I grew up with excitement and chaos. That same night, my father was so drunk he could barely walk, but my mother still allowed him to get behind the wheel. My mother sat next to him, and Val and I were in the back. He started driving north, up Eighteenth Street. There were cars parked on both sides. My father was so drunk, he almost hit every car along the way. My mother had to grab the wheel and steer to prevent my father from hitting parked cars. I was petrified. I sat in the back of my father's dark-green Ford and prayed. With my father's foot on the gas pedal and my mother, who did not know how to drive, steering the car, I held my breath. I do not know how we got home safely that night. When we finally arrived, my mother screamed, hollered, and cursed the entire night. I could not sleep. The next day my mother and father went to work, and I went to school as if nothing had happened.

At age eight, I got my period at a family picnic on Labor Day. The day was cool and breezy. Every year we met in the park with our next-door neighbors and their relatives. When I went to pee in the woods, I saw blood in my panties. I ran and told Val that something was wrong with me. She said, "Tell Mommy." I was scared to tell Mommy. Val was three years older than me and had not gotten her period yet, so she was just as confused as I. Val and I whispered back and forth about what this could possibly be.

"Maybe you will have to go back to the hospital," Valerie said.

I decided to inch my way to my mother to try to get her attention. When I caught her eyes, I whispered in her ear, "I have blood in my panties."

She waved me off and said, "Wait until we get home."

I said to myself, *I might be dead by then.*

Four hours later we came home. I ran upstairs to my bedroom and waited patiently until my mother pushed open the bedroom door, stood in the doorway, and in a fit of rage, threw a blue box of Kotex pads at me and said, "Put these on whenever you see it." That was it. She was infuriated and looked into my eyes with total disgust. I didn't understand why she was so upset with me. I asked myself, "What did I do?" So every time my period came on, I felt ashamed and hated myself. I can remember hating myself from the bottom of my feet up to the top of my head. I couldn't figure out what was so terrible about me.

My mother and father had issues with money. My father got paid on Fridays, but he would not come straight home with the money. I didn't understand why my mother would send me down the street to the corner bar to look for him. I never wanted to go, but she forced me. I was embarrassed and scared to go into the bar. It was a place for adults. Why was my mother sending me in there? I'd run down the street as fast as I could, as if by running fast enough no one would see me. I'd go to the ladies' entrance in the rear and stand at the doorway looking for my father. It was very dark. Martha and the Vandellas's "Heat Wave" was blasting on the jukebox. It was loud and smoky, and my vision was blurry. I looked around the bar and started to focus, and there was my father, dancing and kissing a neighbor, Mrs. Maria. I was devastated and ran home crying.

As soon as I got to my house, my mother was at the door saying, "Did you see him? Was he there?"

I could not tell her what I saw because I was too upset about what I had just seen. My father came in the house two minutes later, and the argument began. It became my responsibility to get my father from the bar whenever he did not come home with the money. My mother would send me to neighbors' homes to retrieve him, and one time I saw him walking around Mrs. Jones's house, a neighbor two doors down from us, going into her refrigerator as if he lived there.

My mother started referring to me as the dirty whore. I'd ask myself, "What is a whore?" Whatever it was, it didn't sound good. It happened whenever I came in from school and she was there. One afternoon she pointed her finger and waved her hands, loudly accusing me of being fondled by little boys. She began yelling, "*Look at your top! It's dirty around your breasts*!"

My breasts developed in the fourth grade, and I was already being teased at school. I remember being very uncomfortable. Grown men approached me as I walked home from school, and I didn't know how to handle this kind of attention. My mother never once asked me if I had homework. Her rage frightened me, and I continued to withdraw, becoming quiet and shy and feeling invisible. My mother berated me daily, and I could do nothing right. Whenever she asked me to do anything, I could never do it to her satisfaction.

Sometimes she would scream at the top of her lungs, "You

are dumb and stupid!" Then she would redo everything I had just spent hours doing while I stood and watched her. I was filled with self-doubt and low self-esteem.

However, school was one the few places I felt safe, and I was able to focus and excel. I was on the honor roll and graduated number ten out of two hundred. Because of my grades, I did an internship and was hired before I graduated.

Author's Afterthoughts

Most of my memories of childhood abuse were submerged until I was thirty five. Yet, I realized later these experiences were directing many of the choices I made in my life. I was committed to healing my trauma. It became my number one priority.

Chapter 2

David

As I was walking to my first job on a crisp fall morning, I met David at Fifteenth and Cumberland streets. I was eighteen years old and felt very grown up. I worked as a librarian at Temple University Paley Library. I was feeling really confident when this nice-looking older man with a mustache called me over to his car. I walked over, and he told me his name was David and asked for mine.

He got out of his car, gave me a hug, and told me, "You still have baby fat." He asked, "What's your number?" I gave him my phone number, and he called me later that same day. We talked for many hours on the phone.

After several months on the phone, he asked me to go for a bike ride on East River Drive. We dated for over a year before I actually called it a relationship. He took me out almost every weekend and introduced me to nightclubs. The Chances Are Club was located at Sixteenth and Locust streets. I walked into this place, and I couldn't take my eyes off the dance floor, which was flashing different colors. It was exciting. He exposed me to many things I had never experienced before. Going out to clubs and being with a gorgeous older man intoxicated me. But slowly over the next two years, David revealed his true colors.

He was a mixture of my parents. He was charming but also critical and never satisfied. I found myself constantly trying to gain his approval. I was willing to allow him to do whatever he wanted to gain his approval. He began controlling me. Two years later, he revealed he had a child and was married.

I asked, "Whose number have I been calling?"

He said, "It's my sister's phone number."

I was very upset and told him it was over. I started using a different route to work and leaving from the rear of the office building at the end of the work day to avoid him. One morning on the way to work, he snuck up behind me and literally picked me up and put me in his car. He put the seat belt around me and told me not to move. I did exactly what he told me to do. Then he took me to the park and raped me. Afterward, he dropped me off at work and pretended nothing had happened. He felt he owned me and that it was his right to have sex with me at any time. I complied. This restarted a five-year relationship of me allowing him to come back and forth. I never questioned his behavior. Not one alarm ever went off in my head. Another time, two months after I was released from the hospital for the removal of my appendix, he came over the next day to visit and forced himself on me, raping me again. He raped me through the pain, raped me through my screams. I was humiliated, and somehow physical and emotional disrespect was acceptable. There were times when I would try to end the relationship, but he would find me and beg and plead for me not to leave him. Because of low self-esteem, I would stay. Our relationship was on and off for most of that time. I really thought this was love.

Before each holiday he would buy me expensive gifts, but when the holidays came, there was no David. I waited for him many times and had anxiety because many times he did not show. My self-esteem was connected to him showing up. When he arrived, I felt great; when he did not, I hated myself and thought there was something wrong with me. He would call early the next morning, or he would be waiting outside to drive me to work the next day. I felt disappointed, but I remained with him anyway.

Four years into my relationship with David, I was still living with my parents, and he didn't like that I had a curfew. He suggested we get an apartment together. I said yes, thinking this would seal our relationship. David gave me money for the apartment, helped purchase furniture, and said he would help with the rent. Within the month I moved into our apartment, very excited. Things started unravel very quickly. When he came home, he was quite upset with me. He complained about my body and the apartment being dirty, and he just was not happy. A month later, he announced, "I'm going back to my wife," and left. He left me with all of the bills, and there were times when I didn't have enough money to buy food, so I went home to my mother's house to eat. I didn't have anywhere left to go. My mother was so upset about me moving out that when I asked for something to eat, she refused and told me not to touch anything in the refrigerator. So I left, and survived on the doughnuts and snacks at work until the next month. I learned how to live on little or no money. I had to learn how to survive. I looked for another job at a bank. My sister was already working there, so she gave me a reference and I was hired.

A couple months later, I called David to come and pick up his belongings, which I had packed up and put at the front door. He didn't come for a while, but then one day he showed up unannounced. He forced his way into the apartment and raped me. The relationship began again. He would come back to me, then leave again. This crazy and abusive relationship continued for a few more years. The thing that finally severed the relationship was me seeing him with another woman who was not his wife in his car. We were traveling in opposite directions on the same road. That was the day that I thought I would end my own life.

I went out with a group of friends and decided to call him after a night of drinking and began asking him to take me back. He said, "Fuck you," and told me that he never wanted to see me again and slammed the phone down. I was so devastated that I started wailing as I sat on the curb in front of the bar at Broad and Girard. After a few hours, my friends came out looking for me, and I was still sitting on the curb crying. They drove me home, and my friend Gloria stayed with me until the next day. When I woke up, I was numb. I knew that I was in trouble. I began to smoke and drink more. My life became a blur. Somehow, I managed to keep my job, but one day flowed into the next as I tried to cope with my broken heart.

I continued to soothe my pain with alcohol until one night I blacked out. In my mind, my life was finished. I had no reason to live, no reason to go on. I drank myself into a haze until I didn't even know where I was. That night, I woke up crying in the middle of the street and didn't remember how I had gotten there. I awakened from a dizzy fog and slowly walked the three blocks back to my apartment. When I reached my apartment, I realized that I had left my front door wide open. This really scared me, and I knew I was spinning out of control. At that moment, I decided to change my life. I stopped drinking and smoking right away. I wrote out goals and put them on the wall and began to make improvements in my life. I enrolled in college at night, and I took self-improvement courses at work.

As I made steps toward my goals, I started to feel better about myself. My self-esteem increased, and my life got better. My mind became clearer, and I actually started asking myself questions. Where was I headed? I wanted to do something different and challenging, so I took every job test I could, including the Philadelphia police test. I tried everything I could to make positive changes in my life.

Author's Afterthoughts

I started putting myself first; by focusing on what I needed and wanted, I was able to make changes in my life.

Chapter 3

Officer O'Malley

The Philadelphia Police Department's written test was administered in a high school in Northeast Philadelphia. I scored 95 percent on the test. As part of the interviewing process, I took a lie detector and psychological test at the police academy. I received notification in the mail that I had passed both tests. The last part was the physical exam. Two weeks later, I reported to MSB building, at Sixteenth and JFK Boulevard in Center City, and met with a doctor who conducted the physical. Finally the doctor instructed me to stand up. He measured my height and said, "Oh, let me measure you again." He did and then said, "You are a quarter of an inch too short." I asked, "Too short for what?" I didn't know there was a height requirement. A month later, I received a letter informing me I did not get the job.

So I returned to my assistant supervisor job at the bank. I was very upset. Three years later, I received a call from someone saying she was from the federal government. She asked if I was Kathleen Morris and asked for my social security number.

"I'm not giving my social security number over the phone," I said.

"Can you can acknowledge if this is your number?" the person asked, as she recited my social security number. "This is the federal government."

"Okay, but I am at work. Can you call me at home?" I asked.

"What time will you be home?" she responded.

I said, "Five thirty." I went home and waited. The phone rang exactly at 5:30 p.m. I answered and asked, "How did you find me?"

She answered, "Your social security number."

Then she told me there was a class action lawsuit against the Philadelphia Police Department for discriminating against women, and my name was on the list. She wanted to confirm I had taken all the tests and my current mailing address. She then asked if I wanted to participate in the lawsuit. I said, "Yes." As part of the settlement, she said, "You will get a job offer and back pay and have seniority. What do you want?"

I said, "I want it all."

It would be a couple of years before I received a letter in the mail telling me to report to the police academy within forty-eight hours. It informed me where to go to purchase my cadet uniform and shoes. This was a shock because I had forgotten completely about it. I had to cut my shoulder-length hair, which I resisted. The commanding officer had to threaten me that if I did not cut my hair I would not graduate from the academy. The physical training was intense, but I was prepared because I was already running four miles a day. Two months into the academy, I was issued a Smith & Wesson Colt 45. I had never seen a gun or been around a weapon before. The gun was too heavy for me. I had to improve my upper body strength to be able to handle it. I started doing chin ups and pushups. After all of the additional self-training, I was able to manage my weapon. When I graduated in the fall, no one in my family celebrated. They attended the ceremony, upset and worried about my safety. My father felt intimidated by me and kept his hands in his pockets while he reminded me he always carried two knives. I ignored him and walked over to my sister, Val, who said, "You would do anything for money." We ate dinner, and I returned to my apartment. There was a message on my home phone instructing me to report to work that night at midnight.

I reported to the Twelfth District at 12:00 a.m. with my gun in its holster and wearing the police-issued uniform designed for a man. I felt invisible as a woman. The clothes were ill fitting and uncomfortable. I had been forced to cut my shoulder-length hair. My femininity had been erased. Arriving to the district, sleepy and scared, Officer Smith came bouncing up to me saying, "I'm your partner tonight. What's your name?" We stood for roll call and were assigned wagon 1202. I got into the wagon with Officer Smith driving, and he went straight to the Wawa for coffee. While waiting in wagon, I heard the radio announcer call, "1202, 1202 domestic dispute." I ran inside and to tell Jimmy, and he said, "Calm down and pace yourself. You will receive many calls during the night. Pace yourself. Slow down." When my partner and I arrived along with two other officers, a man calmly opened the door, and I saw a woman lying on the floor with an ax in her forehead.

I pushed past the man at the door and ran over to the woman, got down on my knees, looked into her eyes, and asked, "Who did this to you?"

She answered, "My husband."

I jumped up with my hand on my gun to go after the husband, who was standing in the room. The other three officers on the scene grabbed me to hold me back while shouting, "Whoa, you got to find out if she wants to press charges."

Kneeling back down, I heard her quietly say, "No, I love my husband."

She would not press charges. Thus began my career as a

police officer. I watched as they carried her out, with the ax still in her head. I was completely devastated. I held on to all of my emotions until I got into my car. I stopped to get a box of donuts, began eating them and cried all the way home.

A couple months later, I was called as the backup during a car stop. As I slowly approached the driver's side of the car, I looked inside the car and saw a gun. Before the driver noticed, I was right there, putting my gun in his ear, instructing him not to move or touch anything. I was relieved that I didn't have to pull the trigger. No one was hurt that day. Still, I never got comfortable with carrying a gun and would leave it in my locker when I left the district at the end of my shift.

After working on the police force for a while, I requested a transfer to be closer to my home and to shorten my commute time. As I walked into the new district, ready for my assignment, an uneasy feeling aroused in my stomach. Not knowing exactly where to go, I looked around and felt hostility in the air. I sat down at the rear of the room thinking that someone would eventually approach me and give me my assignment. As I watched the bustling of activities, people coming in to file complaints, officers preparing for court, I tried to get someone's attention. All of my efforts were ignored. Roll call was announced. I got up and stood in the rear, knowing that the seasoned officers had designated spots. The sergeant would approach each officer and inspect their uniform and weapon. When he got to me, he bypassed me like I was invisible and went to the officer standing next to me. At the end of the roll call, all the officers left for their assignments, and I was left to return to my seat in the back of the room. I knew there would be a second roll call, so I waited. Thirty minutes later, roll call was announced again. I got up to stand for the second roll call. Once again another sergeant approached me, walked right past me, and went to the next officer. I was very confused and attempted to ask someone for help again. No one would speak to me. I was completely ignored. Naively, I thought this was how they treated new officers, but this behavior was very different from how I had been treated in my previous district.

I sat in the seat for another hour, until a blue-eyed Irish veteran officer approached, handed me a walkie-talkie, and told me that he was my partner. I followed him out of the station, and we walked to our assigned sector. He started asking me questions as we walked the beat together. I realized that neither my supervisor nor my squad members wanted anything to do with me. I did not know why. A couple of months later, my new partner began to fill in the blanks. Because I was new and had transferred into the district, they didn't trust me. Everyone in this district avoided me.

Officer O'Malley took me under his wing, and we became fast friends. We started to hang out after work, going to different coffeehouses, and an intimate relationship developed. Because of how I was treated by the other officers, he became overprotective and always wanted to know where I was. I welcomed his concern and felt safe. Soon he began to want to know my every move, on and off duty. I didn't recognize that this behavior was a clear signal of his desire to control me. What once felt like concern began to feel overbearing. Gradually, a tension developed between us.

Since we were an interracial couple, everyone stared when we went out socially. Once when we entered an all-white bar in the greater northeast of Philadelphia, a fight broke out because I was there. I was pushed out of the bar, and he and his buddies fought a mob of angry white men. He rushed out, and we ran to our car, speeding away. I was accustomed to racial tension.

However, he was not. He soon began drinking heavily and grew volatile in our relationship.

Things between us took a downward spiral when the pressures of the job started to mount. O'Malley was consistently being approached with racial slurs about me. They bombarded him with racist comments and sexual innuendo. Eventually I was placed on another sector within the district, and he stayed on his beat. I was reassigned to patrol car 622. I understood I was in the middle of a pressure cooker—a hostile environment. One night while on patrol, I received a call: "Man with a gun." I said, "622, okay," and I heard my backup answer, "613, okay." Since I did not trust my fellow officers, I decided not to be the first officer on the scene. As I circled the block, I saw my backup officers circling the block as well. I realized my backup did not have any intention of backing me up, and I decided to report on the radio the call was unfounded. I never did find out if the call was real. I felt alone, and my life was in jeopardy.

One year later, O'Malley asked me to marry him. He bought me an engagement ring, and we purchased a house together in Fairmount section of Philadelphia. Two weeks after I moved in, O'Malley became abusive and starting using racial slurs. One day, I was asleep on the third floor, after working the midnight shift. O'Malley burst into the room, grabbed me by my T-shirt, and lifted me up out of the bed. I started punching back and ran out of the house. On my way out, I was shocked to see that he had broken all of my glass tables on the first floor. Secretly, I began looking for an apartment.

I started sleeping in the living room fully dressed after that incident. His drinking became more and more out of control. One evening, months later, O'Malley announced, "Do not to leave the house." I didn't take him seriously because we needed food, so I put on my coat and continued on my way. When I returned a couple of hours later with groceries, he was sitting on the couch with a half-empty bottle of Jack Daniels whiskey and his gun on the table.

He looked directly into my eyes and whispered, "I'm going to kill you tonight" as he poured another drink.

I responded by saying, "Stop playing around. Don't be ridiculous."

I got up from the sofa, went into the kitchen, and got my favorite chocolate from the refrigerator. He said, "That chocolate's not going to help you. I'm going to make it so that even your own mother won't recognize you." I looked up at him and finally realized that he was serious. He had a blank stare in his eyes—the kind of stare that lets you know that evil is in the room. A cold chill went up my spine. He picked up his gun, pointed it at me, and said, "I told you not to leave the house."

Survival mode kicked in, and I decided not to run for the door. I slowly got up from the couch and looked directly into his eyes and backed up the stairs Not once did I take my eyes away from his. Once upstairs, in the third-floor bedroom, I planned my escape. I decided if I heard him coming up the stairs, I would hide on the roof deck.

All my friends and family had abandoned me because I was with this white guy. I did not trust the police. I decided to call a childhood girlfriend of mine—Debbie—whom I had not spoken with in five years. I told her what happened, and she said to come to her home as soon as I could.

I stayed awake the entire night. I left the next day at dawn. O'Malley was knocked out in a drunken stupor on the sofa as I tiptoed out. It was Thanksgiving Day. I went to work my shift, and then I went to my sister's house for dinner. When I got to her house, I ran upstairs, hid in a corner, and cried. My family asked what was wrong. I told them what happened, and they convinced me to file a Protection from Abuse document against him. I left the house and drove directly to the roundhouse (police headquarters). Once there, the administrative officer told me to sit in his office while he talked to the judge. I sat there and cried. I was in full uniform, feeling humiliated and embarrassed. With the signed documents, I returned to Debbie's house. I needed to go and get my clothes. Debbie convinced me to have a police escort meet me there. The policeman rang the doorbell while I hid behind a large parked truck. I was terrified. O'Malley opened the door to police officers he knew. He commenced to joking and laughing, saying, "You know how women are," acting as if nothing had even happened. I was scared, running around the house throwing everything in green plastic trash bags. I took only what could fit into my car. I naively thought it would be the last time I'd see O'Malley.

From that day forward, he stalked me while I was at work and off duty. Two weeks after I left, I noticed a car following me. Alarmed, I sped up and went thorough stop signs and traffic lights. I looked into my rearview mirror, and the same car was still behind me. I quickly pulled behind a large truck, and the vehicle zoomed in front of me. I started following the car and wrote the license tag down. When I got to work, I ran the tag. I discovered I needed a special clearance to get more information. I was continuously on edge, always looking over my shoulders, thinking that one day O'Malley might succeed in taking my life. I began to have night terrors. I woke up screaming, standing in front of my bedroom wall. I was sleepwalking. The next time I woke up, I was standing at the windows, nude. I had become an emotional and mental wreck.

I decided to seek counseling and redirected my attention to survival and moving forward. Although he stalked me for years, leaving threatening notes on my car, I refused to give in and allow his behavior to control me. For a long time my furniture and belongings were left in the house. It took years of legal action to sell the house and for me to get some of my belongings back. I was grateful I had survived.

Author's Afterthoughts

I learned that the universe is always working for my highest good. I learned my life has value and life is worth living. I learned just because you made a decision, it doesn't mean you can't change your mind. I almost lost my life because I wanted to keep my word. I learned O'Malley wanting to know where I was at all times was not love but control.

As soon as you feel disrespected in any way, walk away and don't turn around. Love does not hurt.

Chapter 4

Enter the Caribbean/ Winston Williams

A few years later, after working the 4:00 p.m. to midnight shift, I went to a local night spot and met a man from the Caribbean. I had decided to go out for fun. I saw Winston from across the room—a tall, hard-bodied man with light-brown eyes and sweet-potato-brown skin. He came over to me and asked, "May I have this dance please?" extending his hand. I said yes and took his hand as we both walked toward the dance floor. He started swaying his hips back and forward in rhythm to the music.

He asked, "What's your name?"

I answered, "Kathy."

He said, "I'm Winston."

We both smiled. He then asked for my phone number. He called me the next day and asked me out to dinner. We talked on the phone often. Winston was considerate, respectful, and kind, and being with him felt different. I felt uncomfortable. He kept his word by showing up when he said he would. He spent time with me, took me out to dinner and movies. We also went to Caribbean concerts. I was so accustomed to men not showing up and leaving me hanging that I didn't know how to respond to him initially. However, my heart got the best of me, and I opened up to his love.

After six months of dating, I decided to help Winston start a small auto repair business. Winston was always complaining about his salary from his construction job. I said to him, "The only way to build wealth is to start your own business."

I made a financial investment to help him purchase tools and business cards. Every Sunday we sat at our kitchen table and made plans for the business. We enjoyed working together. My background in business administration and his ambition were a great combination. After two years, he asked for my hand in marriage. I immediately became anxious about a wedding because of my family. My mother, Edith, and my father, Eric, were both heavy drinkers. Actually, everyone in my immediate family drank, and I didn't want to be embarrassed by them, so we decided to get quietly married by a Justice of the Peace in Upper Darby, PA. I wore a matching black-and-white polka dot top and skirt, and Winston wore a beige suit. We celebrated by going to Tobin's seafood restaurant in West Oak Lane section of Philly. I didn't want any family drama around this loving relationship. After several months, we moved to a large three-bedroom apartment in West Philly, at Forty-Fifth and Walnut Street.

We expanded the business by purchasing another building and establishing a second location. As we put more time and energy into the business, it started to grow. The success of the business strengthened the relationship. For the first time, I felt safe. I felt great, and at the same time I recognized my growing feelings of insecurity. Our relationship blossomed. I loved knowing that there was someone in my life who cared about me. He showered me with gifts. One Valentine's Day he left a card on my pillow, flowers, and candles lit on the bedroom dresser. Despite all of the happiness, I felt I didn't deserve him.

Two years into my marriage, I was hit by the car and placed on disability. This drastically changed our relationship. I walked around with a cane, in pain, and became depressed. I was used to being active, and now I was at home staring up at the ceiling. To distract myself, I read books. With time on my hands, my mind raced back to my past abusive relationships. I felt damaged inside. I began to examine my life. At nineteen years old, I was kidnapped and raped by David. At twenty-nine, O'Malley pointed gun at me, threatening to kill me. The more I thought about these relationships, I was afraid they would impact my marriage.

Two weeks later while reading the newspaper, I noticed an advertisement for a study group for the book, *Women Who Love Too Much*. The book was about dysfunctional relationships and an explanation of why those relationships are tolerated. In order to become a member of this group, you had to read the first three chapters. I read the entire book and knew right away that this book was all about me and my life. I could not wait until the group got started.

I had never been in group therapy before and had no idea what to expect. Five women from different backgrounds and I committed to meet for at least six months. We met once a week. I sat in that room week after week, hearing stories; they were my story. I felt understood and relieved. Because my past relationships had been so abusive, I worked hard within the group to gain a better understanding of my past and learn what I needed to change. I began to make connections to group members, and for the first time, I felt supported.

About three years into marriage, and about six months into group therapy, my husband took me to see the movie *Nuts*, starring Barbara Streisand. There was a scene in the movie where the woman's father slipped money to her while she was taking a bath. Right at that instant my mind flashed to my father bathing me when I was about four years old. I remembered feeling uncomfortable with my father, Eric, being in the bathroom. Sitting in the movie theater with my eyes glued to the screen, a frightened and confused feeling came over me. I had never had a flashback before in my life. It was a flash but etched in my memory. I kept returning to the flash, asking, "Why would he be bathing me?" Denial would kick in, and I would push it out of my head. Still, I was shaken to my core. I said nothing about this to my husband, but I called the group therapist the next day in tears, wondering why I was so upset. The group therapist suggested that I begin individual therapy.

In therapy I remembered him bathing me, and immediately I told myself that my mind was playing tricks on me. This flashback of being touched in between my legs by my father in the bathtub played over and over in my mind. I began an investigation. I asked my mother, "Why was he bathing me?" I was old enough to bathe myself. The same question came up many times. Why was he bathing me? Why was he touching me between my legs? My mother told me, *no*, that didn't happen. So I told myself, "No, Kathy, that did not happen. You are losing your mind. Your father would never do anything like that to you." I kept repeating that same message over and over to myself and to my therapist.

Thoughts of being touched sexually by my father dominated my thoughts. To ease the pain and fear, I started eating. I would go shopping secretly for food after my husband left for work. I bought Snyder's of Hanover hard pretzels and Lay's potato chips. They became my secret lovers during the day. I also got coffee with extra cream and sugar. Now I had a complete ménage a trois. I ate until exhaustion and went to sleep. I threw away any evidence of my binge eating from my husband. This pattern continued until I noticed I had gained a considerable amount of weight. My size ballooned, and before I knew it, I puffed up from a size eight to a size sixteen. I hated myself for gaining weight. Why did I have wear my pain on the outside?

I saw a commercial on TV one day, and it said, "It's not what you are eating; it's what's eating you. Call this eight hundred number." I picked up the telephone and called right away. A counselor answered, and I immediately began to cry. I told her my story of binge eating and how it was destroying my life. I was convinced that my husband would leave or that I would kill myself. She convinced me this program could help me, and I decided to go into treatment for food addiction. This pattern of overeating had followed me from my childhood into adulthood, and I wanted to get to find out why I was using food to cope with stress. The program flew me into Las Vegas for twenty-nine days. While I was away, I gained insight about how food stops me from feeling. With the new controlled diet, a barrage of emotions came up.

I began to piece together actual accounts of sexual abuse by my father. These memories were traumatic. Shame became my best friend, and I asked myself, "Why this did happen to me?"

Being in treatment in Las Vegas helped me to retrieve intense memories, and the help of the treatment center staff allowed me to feel some of the grief and lost innocence in my childhood. I was able to experience letting go of some of the pain. I knew I had plenty more.

When I came home thirty days later, part of my outpatient treatment plan was to go to Incest Survivors Anonymous (ISA) meetings, and also continued therapy twice a week.

I called my father, and asked "Why did you touch me?"

He said in a sweet voice, "I would never harm you."

I believed him, even after what I had been through in Las Vegas with some memories surfacing of being touched inappropriately by him; I wanted it not to be true. I dismissed my memories and went back into denial, but I became extremely depressed after that conversation with my father. My mother had also said that that could never happen. I didn't have a clue as to what to do next.

It became increasingly difficult to be married. Our union as husband and wife began slowly crumbling upon my return from treatment in Las Vegas. I never shared with him what was going on with me. I never told him I was struggling with shame and eating so much food not to face the truth, stuffing my feelings down. I never told him I didn't want to be touched and felt violated by even his hugs. Memories came when my husband approached me for sex. I felt as if I were being raped, and sometimes I would even see my father's face over Winston's. I didn't want to be touched sexually. Winston's sexual advances toward me often ended with me crying uncontrollably. He was impatient and confused because we'd had a healthy sexual life before the first flashback. Different flashbacks were happening on a regular basis, and more memories of me giving my father oral sex were surfacing. I kept seeing my father sexually abusing me. My husband did not understand why I had changed. I kept secrets.

Secrets and depression slowly dissolved our loving relationship. I stopped talking to him and began isolating in the back room of our home. When he came home from work, I would be sleeping and didn't want to get up and engage him. Finally, after he demanded to know what was going on with me, I took him to my therapist to explain. Winston did not believe my father had sexually abused me. He had developed a close relationship with Eric and refused to think he was capable of such atrocities. I could not look my husband in the eyes. I felt ashamed, and I believed that he would reject me because I was damaged goods. Two years later, we separated and divorced. I became aware at that time he was involved with someone else, and frankly I understood. I asked him to leave our home and said, "This is not a marriage." I felt anger and rage, and all I could see was pain, deceit, and betrayal.

After the divorce, I stopped going to all forms of therapy. I needed some time just to be. In order to save money, Val and I decided to get an apartment together, and we moved to a large apartment in East Falls, Philadelphia. At first being with my sister felt great, but after eight months I began feeling emotionally upset again. Also, Val started working for the government, and it required her to travel most of the time. With Val not being around, feelings of depression and anxiety prevailed. I started looking for another therapist. Through a referral from a good friend, I met a new therapist. By the time I met her, I was sitting in her office lobby, crying on the day of my first appointment. I was a mess. We met, and she was not shaken by my emotions. She was able to calm me down.

After several sessions with this new therapist, I had another flashback. Now I wanted to kill myself. I remembered having a miscarriage when I was eight years old. There was blood everywhere, on the sheets, in the bed, on my clothes. Even when I got to school, there was blood on my skirt and on my gym suit. That memory was extremely vivid. I asked my older sister Val about it, and she said, "Yes I remember that morning with all the blood." I was shocked at her response. I thought that she'd say it was all in my mind; but here she was, validating my memories. That shook me to my core. Everything within me wanted to shut down and die. I could not believe it. I did not want to believe it.

My binge eating returned. I could not get enough potato chips and pretzels into my body to push down the pain and the hurt that I felt. I just wanted to die. I was in my new therapist's office twice a week, and she wanted me to give her a verbal contract that I would not kill myself, but I could not do that. I wanted to kill myself. She wanted to admit me into the hospital. At first I refused. I sat in my bedroom with shades drawn in my dark brown pajamas with tears streaming down my face, contemplating jumping out of my second-floor window, head first. I only wanted to die to end the pain, and I saw no other way out. My therapist was so concerned about me she called my sister Val, who was upstairs. Val knocked on my bedroom door and slowly opened it and looked in. She walked in, sat on my bed, and took the covers from over my head. I told her I couldn't do it anymore. My life was over. She took my hand and reassured me that it was not my fault and convinced me to go to the hospital. Val drove me to Belmont Behavioral Hospital, and I was admitted. While there, I worked through some of the issues of being impregnated by my father at eight years old. My therapist came to visit me at the hospital, and I felt supported. I was introduced to art and pottery at this program and noticed how soothing it was to use my hands. I stayed for twenty-eight days.

This time when I got out of the hospital, I decided to confront the family again, stating if they did not accept that I had been abused, then they could not accept me. They absolutely could not accept that I had been abused by my father, and so I broke off all communication with my family except for Val. It was a difficult thing for me to do. I changed my phone number and worked my outpatient treatment plan by going to my therapist, the twelve-step programs, and my support network. It was more important than ever.

I was able to work beyond some of the emotional pain. I told everyone I met that I had been sexually abused by my father. I now walked with a sense of freedom. I didn't want to keep any more secrets.

Author's Afterthoughts

I learned that love frightened me. It was the first time I worked together with a man as a unit, and I blossomed. I felt good being in a relationship. I learned to be interdependent. It had been difficult for me to learn to depend and trust someone. I learned to compromise. He taught me how to demonstrate love. I learned how to forgive.

Chapter 5

Jamaica

I was still walking with a cane. The pain from my auto accident felt worse in the winter months. My leg ached like a toothache, and I would hobble around with my cane. One day Diane, my best friend, was under so much stress from her job, she told me, "I want to break my boss's neck."

I responded, "Maybe you might need to take a vacation."

She mentioned how much she loved Jamaica. I said, "Jamaica sounds about right."

So we made the arrangements to go to Jamaica. We left in February, in the middle of a very cold winter, the temperature hovering around fifteen degrees. I had been out of the hospital for sixteen months. We were bundled up and dressed with many layers. Diane wore two pairs of sweatpants, and I had on two hoodies and one sweater.

I asked her on the plane, "Are we on our way to the North Pole?" We both laughed so hard and loud that everyone on the plane started laughing with us. I was so ecstatic to be traveling to some warm place in the middle of winter. It was something I thought only rich people could do.

When I arrived in Jamaica, I felt a deep connection to the land. I felt as if I were returning home. Immediately my soul began to relax. I knew I was meant to be there. Looking out on the horizon, I felt connected to the creator. With my feet in the white sand and spending time in the crystal-clear waters, I felt grateful. I never imagined myself doing something like this. My heart smiled. I was happy. I felt nurtured by nature. It was magical. A few days ago I had been in the bitter cold, dressed like a polar bear, and now I was sitting in the Caribbean Sea in a bathing suit.

I was in deep gratitude. I wrote in a journal, read, created art at the edge of the ocean, and meditated in prayer. Healing was happening, I noticed my physical healing right away. My legs and back felt better. The sun, sand, and relaxation helped me to feel better; it was exactly what I needed.

On the sixth day, we reluctantly packed and went to the airport. When we arrived at the airport the ticket agent informed us that the East Coast had been unexpectedly hit with a snowstorm and no planes could land in Philadelphia. We could not leave the island. God had a hand in extending our vacation for another three days. Diane and I laughed all the way back to the hotel and sat in the lobby sipping Jamaican Blue Mountain Coffee. We put our bathing suits back on and went back to the beach. We left three days later.

When I returned to Philadelphia, I realized I did not need my cane as much. Our spirits were so high that Diane and I decided to return to Jamaica two months later. I began to go to Jamaica on a regular basis and stayed in the same apartment located directly across from the beach.

While I was sitting in the ocean, and looking out at the horizon, a tall, handsome Jamaican man with swimmer's shoulders came up to me. He asked, "Did you see that shark?"

I looked up with panic in my eyes, looking around, saying, "Where? Where?"

When I looked back at him, he was laughing. He chuckled and said, "I was only kidding."

We both laughed so hard. He sat down next to me on the shore and began a conversation that lasted two hours. He worked nearby on a boat that took tourists on cruises around the island. His name was Carlton, and when he left, I hoped I would see him on the beach again. I saw him the next day, and he invited me out on a date. That night after work, I waited in the lobby of the Fantasy Hotel wearing a yellow and gold sun dress. He walked with a swagger, wearing a pair of jeans that hugged every part of his body. I got excited with each step he took. He walked up and said, "Kathy, you look beautiful tonight."

I smiled and said, "Thank you. Where are we going?" We went to a rooftop pub with outdoor lighting. I became mesmerized with the surroundings. It was very crowded with a mixture of people, some locals but mostly tourists from England. I blocked out everyone and everything and only saw the stars and heard the melodic sound of Carlton's voice. We talked and swayed to music until 3:00 a.m. We loved spending time with each other. He became a huge support to me whenever I came to Jamaica.

I hated to return back home to the States because I felt emotionally and physically better in Jamaica. My injuries responded well in the warm climate, so I decided to move to Jamaica. Carlton helped me find an apartment. I had the ocean at my feet every day. He came by frequently to visit and help me navigate my new surroundings. He taught me how to get around on the transportation system and how to shop at the outdoor market for food. I started to settle down rather quickly due to the fact I had been coming back and forth for six months.

He was fun and loved to cook. He introduced me to his friend Donald, who had a girlfriend, Maria, from New York, and we all hung out at different night spots on the island. We rented a car and took a two-hour day trip to Negril and ate at

Rick's café. Carlton often invited me, Donald, and Maria on the boat to cruise around the island. Maria and I became friends and often ate breakfast and went shopping while Donald and Carlton worked. Every Sunday Carlton would cook on the boat and then take it out for a cruise; we sat in the middle of the ocean listening to Bob Marley. I was in utter and complete happiness. I put the traumas of the abuse on the back burner. I sat in the ocean and purged my emotions through tears and prayer. I'd spend most of my time outdoors. I did things in Jamaica I had never done before. I rode on a private boat and learned to swim.

After four months of bliss, I received several calls from my bank in Philadelphia. I realized I had to clear up this situation in person. All of my bills were being paid automatically from my checking account and because of a technical problem had stopped. I had to return to the United States. I said my good-byes and flew home within a week and went directly to the bank. The bank needed a signature and immediately fixed the problem.

Once I was home, I felt different. I was stronger physically and mentally. The pain I had experienced before I left had subsided. I felt brand new on the outside and inside.

As I walked down South Street, I began to sense people's emotions and stories. It was confusing to me at first. I had a glimpse into their lives. It was too much to handle, so I sought help of a tribal healer. I arrived at the healer's apartment, parted red fabric, and entered; her walls were covered with maps from around the world.

We sat on pillows on the floor; she spoke very slow and asked, "Where were you? What body of water was near?"

I said, "The Caribbean Sea." She described to me what she thought had happened. She said I experienced a "walk in" from the sea, a healing and gift from the ocean. My intuition had been magnified.

Author's Afterthoughts

I learned from being in Jamaica that I could survive and even thrive in a different country. Being in nature increased my creativity. Jamaica was a divine destiny for me. I grew by leaps and bounds and returned home a different person.

Chapter 6

Rebirthing

Although I had been in traditional therapy for a long time, I continued to feel out of balance. I knew intuitively that I needed something more intense than traditional therapy. I felt restless and wanted to propel myself into a deeper level of healing. A spiritual advisor suggested I try a technique that eliminated spoken word and bypassed the intellect. She highly recommended rebirthing. I got the name of a rebirther from a friend, called, and immediately set up an appointment.

Rebirthing became a pivotal fork in the road as part of my healing process. I was feeling scared and uneasy but hopeful as I began this new journey. The sessions consisted of one hour of talking and one hour of deep consciousness breathing. Deep consciousness breathing, called cleansing breaths, required breathing in through the nose and then out of the mouth. The very minute I started the circular breathing, I experienced deep, intense memories. My entire body shook, and immediately I was certain this experience would be different. With rebirthing the memories were crystal clear, like watching a movie in my mind. Up until this point, I only had flashes or small glimpses of a scene. This experience put on notice that I could no longer deny or hide in the shadows. I always had doubts, somehow thinking I made everything up. Now I began to realize without any doubt that my father had sexually abused me. I remembered being beaten, choked, and raped like an animal. His behavior was very confusing because by day he was a loving father, and at night he was a rapist.

On many occasions I felt close to death. My father rode me like a grown woman. He forced his penis inside many parts of me. He put his hand over my mouth so I would not scream. In order to survive, I consciously left my body and pretended to be someone else and somewhere else.

These new memories were very disturbing. I saw my father come into my bedroom, pick me up, and take me to the basement. I was six. When I resisted, the violence started. He pushed me down the basement steps and beat me. While raping me, he would press his forearm on my throat. I was repeatedly thrown down the basement steps, choked, and raped. There was a deep, empty feeling in the pit of my heart. I felt trapped and spiritually destroyed. I had no sense of myself. I felt hopeless.

I remembered at the age eight, I had trouble fitting into my clothes. My mother never wanted to buy me new ones. I remembered having trouble fitting into a Sunday dress. I had to lay down on the bed while my sister Val tried to zip it up. My weight continued to increase, especially around the age of thirteen. I cried most mornings because I had clothes in my closet, but nothing fit. The simple daily tasks were traumatic.

I remember getting up early in the morning to sneak food and candy. I hid cookies inside the dining room closet. Many times my father would surprise me in the closet, forcing me to perform oral sex. I also remember looking into the dining room mirror and seeing my mother watching us from the top of the stairs.

Because of the abuse, I felt invisible and believed I was there for others and not for myself. Being seen meant pain. There was plenty of pain, tears, and blood. Through the rebirthing sessions, I started to remember all of the details. I became suicidal, and death seemed easier than acknowledging all of these memories.

To cope with my feelings, I began binge eating. Overeating was an old friend, and I was out of control again. I ate huge amounts of food to cover up feelings of shame and guilt. I had to focus my attention on overeating and feeling uncomfortable in my body to continue to live. I felt ashamed and dirty. My rebirthing coach told me about spiritual bathing. After the sessions I would take longs baths with sea salt and baking soda. Sometimes I would take two baths a day because the water was very soothing.

I recalled several new memories of having oral sex with my father, and this bothered me greatly. I became so nervous and out of control that I started obsessively brushing my teeth and washing my hands. These patterns became so prevalent that eventually I could not leave the house. I felt crazy. I thought people could see the semen on me. I felt like a dumping ground and a cesspool. I did not want to be seen.

No matter what I did, I woke up with thoughts of killing myself. These feelings were so intense I thought I would be in therapy forever, so I increased my rebirthing sessions.

My rebirthing coach told me something that would change everything around. She said I could never physically wash off the memories. The abuse had been a long time ago, and I could never wash off the residue. I was trying to wash away what happened. I felt dirty from the deepest part of my soul. My father's semen was in every part of my body, and no amount of bathing, teeth brushing, or hand washing could ever change that. I needed to heal my broken heart. I cried throughout the entire two-hour session. I cried so much the tears stained my face, but I think the crying helped cleanse my soul. My emotions came from a deeper level. The coach explained I was healing at a deeper level. I was actually getting better.

I continued the baths and began to recite positive affirmations. I practiced forgiveness exercises by writing affirmations of forgiveness seventy times a day for seven days.

Affirmations: This feeling is a memory. I can trust myself now. I am only remembering in order to heal. I am getting better now. The memories are safe to feel. I can breathe now.

I began to honor my healing process. Once a week, I would show up for the sessions and work my way through deep-seated memories. Somehow, through the pain, tears, and suicidal thoughts, I managed to look into the eyes of the coach and knew she cared about me and my healing. I began to trust her. She told me to write and repeat affirmations. I followed her instructions to the letter. She was my only hope. She told me if I worked through these painful memories, I could climb out of this abyss.

It's okay to go through this process because I am healing. I will let love and not fear run my life and choices. My word is filled with good people. It is safe to be here, no matter what I am feeling.

I learn to present during remembering. Take a deep breath. The more I breathe, the more I let go.

During most of the healing process, the rebirthing coach pulled me along kicking and screaming. She announced one day that she would no longer pull me along. She said I needed to take control and volunteer to heal myself. At first I was upset, because I relied heavenly on her faith and knowledge to carry me forward. I had never felt so respected and cared for in a therapy environment. I called her my guardian angel and gave her credit for saving my life. Without her wisdom and assistance, I would not be alive today. Now it was time for me to step up to the plate. Have faith in the process, and put into practice what I learned working with her.

Affirmations: There is a difference between surrendering and giving up. It is safe to feel anger now. I love my anger. It teaches me and heals me. It is safe to feel my feelings now. Nothing bad will happen. My terror is in the past, though it feels real right now. There is nothing wrong with me even when I think so.

There would be no more emotional roller coaster or lying in bed. I kept reminding myself I was okay. I had survived the healing as well.

Author's Afterthoughts

I learned the abuse had cut me to my core, and yet it shaped me. I learned I have a deep willingness to face my darkest fear because I wanted to heal. This stripped away my ego and took me to the lowest places. I had to rise up from the ashes like a phoenix. I was at minus ninety-nine and the healing brought me up to zero. I learned I have something to say, something to give, and I want to assist others to do what I have done. I want to be a hand holder to help others turn around and face their fears. I want to share all the tools I used during my healing journey. I also learned that healing looks and feels scary, but the insanity must be torn down in the soul and then rebuilt with love.

Chapter 7

Daddy's Sunday Ties

There came a time in my therapy when my wrists became the focus. I always had fear associated with my wrists and never understood why. There were dark memories buried within my wrists.

Daddy used his beautiful Sunday ties to restrain me. Why, Daddy, why? "Be quiet, baby, I'm not going to hurt you," he would say. He wanted to make sure I would still be in the basement whenever he came back. It was dark, and the cement floor was cold. I stared up at the exposed pipes on the ceiling. I was trapped and alone and had nowhere to turn. The silence was deafening; I looked down and noticed the beautiful colors of the ties—blue, yellow, and red—wrapped around my wrists. How could he use something so beautiful to do something so awful? By the time he came back to the basement, we both had blank stares. My spirit left my body and moved to the ceiling. His spirit left his body. Our spirits met on the ceiling. Totally detached, I watched from the ceiling as if I were watching a movie.

I tried my best to squeeze my legs together really tight, so he could not penetrate me, but he mounted me as if I were a woman. The pain shot through my entire body. I wanted to scream, but my fear kept me silent. I remained quiet and did exactly what I was told. I stopped fighting after a while because it was useless. I learned that I could not win. He won. He was on top. He was in complete control—my father during the day, a rapist at night.

Remembering this particular scene brought back a flood of tears. Being restrained is one of my deepest fears. Do not block me. Do not block my way. I am always looking for a way out or a way to escape. For a long time I did not remember being tied up. Throughout the years, I was aware only that I had pain around my wrists. I rubbed my wrists constantly.

I remember lying in the basement of our house looking up and waiting for the terror to start. I knew what was coming, and I had time to prepare myself mentally, leaving my body, coming back, leaving my body, and coming back again. Sometimes, after he had finished and when he untied me, I stayed in the dark basement, staring into space. I was unable to move, afraid to move; it was my fault. This happened over and over again.

I spent much of my childhood staring into space. My mind could not focus on anything other than surviving, staying alive, and existing. My entire body shook, and immediately I was certain that this experience would be drastically different from all of my other therapy sessions. These new memories were clearly identifiable and concise. It was the first time that I received undeniable information about the sexual abuse I had suffered. Before, I had only glimpses.

I no longer could doubt that my father had severely sexually abused me.

Bathing had become a ritual that I began to look forward to. In fact, I spent most of my time in the bathtub, and that helped tremendously. I also began to recite positive affirmations that were given to me by the rebirther, I would repeat, "There is nothing wrong with me." I thought there was something wrong with me due to the treatment I received as a child. I was on a healing journey.

I started feeling comfortable in sharing my story. I went public by sharing my story in small groups. In one of these groups, a writer from a national magazine asked to publish my story. My story appeared, and I received calls from around the country praising me for having the courage to speak out.

Author's Afterthoughts

Even though I thought I was falling apart, I was actually healing. I learned to respect the process and to express my emotions in the moment. When I was happy, I laughed. When I sad, I cried.

Chapter 8

Changing of the Guard

As my parents grew older, I started taking care of them. This was another learning experience about my capacity to love and to forgive. Three months after my article came out, I received a call from my mother's doctor. She explained a spot had showed up on my mother's chest X-ray. I didn't understand why the doctor called.

I asked, "Why are you calling me?"

She answered, "Because your mother will need support."

"Support for what?" I asked, not comprehending the message the doctor was trying to give me. *Break it down gently*, I thought to myself.

"Your mother has a spot on her lung," the doctor repeated.

"What does that mean?" I asked again.

She answered, "It may be cancer. When I make the appointment for your mother, make sure that you come with her." When I hung up the telephone, I felt fear, and I cried.

Within a month of the call, we visited the doctor. The appointment created fear for both me and my mother. I wanted to find a hole and crawl inside. I went to bed and woke up afraid. I wanted to be strong in order to support her, but a large part of me wanted to break down and fall apart.

With each doctor's appointment, I saw my mother become increasingly vulnerable. The visits also revealed intimate details of my mother's health. She grew increasingly combative with her doctor. At subsequent visits she began crying. I tried to comfort her but did not know how. This was the first time I had ever seen my mother frightened. I never imagined my mother could be afraid.

As time went on, I began to feel a connection with her. There was a sadness surrounding my mother. She had reached the point where she no longer wanted to live, and she stayed on the sofa most of the time. I began taking care of her daily needs. I felt a changing of the guard.

At one point while taking care of my mother, I became extremely upset and emotional. This felt final. I wanted to say so many things, and yet I had nothing to say. I wanted to do so many things but could not do anything. There were so many words on the tip of my tongue, and yet there was nothing more for me say. I don't even know how to describe how I felt. I was dealing with the loss of a mother I'd never had.

What I wanted to say had nothing to do with what was happening but had everything to do with her leaving. There was a part of me leaving and a part of me that I was gaining. I had to hold myself together, even though I wanted to fall apart.

I wanted to know why my mother wasn't there for me. I wanted to know why she allowed my father to hurt me. Why did she allow him to hurt her? Why didn't she love me? Why did she leave me? Why did she give birth to me? Why was she leaving me now, with all of these unanswered questions?

As my mother laid on her deathbed, she watched my father leave the house with two beers in his hands to drink on the front steps with another woman. Her pain permeated the house. Everyone present felt it. She never once screamed out, and she did not ask for pain medicine. It was left up to me to decide when to give it to her.

I did not want to face the fact that she and I would never rectify our relationship. I would not recognize full forgiveness until well after her death. Even now it is hard for me to understand what really happened between us. I never understood why she left me with Daddy. How could she watch in silence and let him repeatedly rape me? Why did it have to take most of my life to gather parts of myself, to become somewhat whole?

I watched my mother and wondered how we got to this point without resolution. I wanted answers, and I wanted closure.

I began to think back to our session at her therapist's office. I asked my mother to go to therapy with me after the article came out. She was very upset about me airing the family business in public. She did agree to go. She sat near the therapist. I sat farther away. The therapist asked me to tell my mother all of the things my father did to me. As I told my story, I knew in the back of my mind that she knew what I was going to say. Still, I told it.

I was aware that she would not be able to handle my accusation that she "knew." She was fragile. It took everything in her power to show up at those sessions. It took an enormous act of love. It took everything in her to stand there with her dignity intact and say that she was sorry for the things that happened to me. It took great courage.

However, I believe my mother allowed her self-blame to eat her alive with the cancer. I saw in her eyes the years of pain, hurt, and guilt. I spent many days and nights asking her questions about her life. I wish now that I had taped some of those conversations. I wish that I could hear her voice again. I wish that I could see her face one more time. She died within two years of the phone call. There is a time in life when you know that unfolding events will change you forever. This is that time. My mother is dying, and it is having an effect on me that I did not expect. On September 5, 1999, my mother died.

Chapter 9

Taking Care of My Elderly Father

Six months after my mother died, I took my father to the bank. When my father stood in line for the teller, I sat in the lobby. I looked over and noticed he was wearing a brown shoe on the right foot and a black shoe on the left. This was the first time I noticed his inability to dress himself. I knew I had to play a larger role in taking care of him. I realized that he would not be here forever. I began to call and visit my father more often. This was really difficult because my father allowed women of questionable character in the house. I took him shopping and to the doctor and made sure the bills got paid.

I was always worried about my father, never knowing what he was doing. One time I called him and he didn't answer the phone, so later that day I called again. So I waited two days and called again, and again, no answer. The next day I went to his house, and he wasn't there. He was missing for two weeks, along with all the money from his bank account. Neighbors would call and tell me my father was hanging outside of the house in his underwear or that he had a house full of people drinking.

My father always did exactly what he wanted to do regardless of consequences, so I sat him down and told him I was taking control of his money. I bought papers from the bank and had him sign all accounts over to me. I had all monies funneled through one bank, which paid the bills and then sent some money to my father's account, so he could have pocket money. For the next four years—which felt like any eternity—I lovingly took care of my father. Every doctor's visit I was on edge, due to his constant drinking, but he always walked away with a clean bill of health and a great attitude. During a doctor's visit the doctor asked him, "Who is the president"? My father could not remember.

Several months later I received a call from him, telling me he was not feeling well. I went to pick him up and took him to Temple Hospital emergency ward. We sat in the lobby, and with each hour that went by, he became more confused. So here I sat with my father, having to restrain him and then taking him to the bathroom. I was so traumatized having to deal with his penis when I first came into the world and now dealing with it when he was on his way out. I wanted someone to come and help me. After twelve hours they finally admitted him into the hospital.

Going home that night, I cried the whole way. I knew something was wrong with him; after all, he was eighty-eight years old. Two days later I went to visit him. When I arrived, he sat up in the bed and said, "God is good" and "I know what I did to you was not right, but I was drunk. I'm sorry." He also added that he felt I was his protector. I was speechless. First of all I had never heard my father speak of God and now an apology. His doctor asked to speak to me privately; we went into a conference room. My heart was pounding, and I thought I heard the doctor say something about cancer had spread from his liver, to his heart and now brain. The doctor continued to say that he would be transferred to hospice in a few days. I felt completely lost. I left and started making plans for his death. He was transferred to hospice the next day; I was right by his side the entire time. Once he left the hospital, he lapsed into a coma. I felt complete with him and was glad I could assist with his transition. My father died in April of 2004.

To My Father, What I miss About You
Even though you hurt me to my core,
I still miss you.
I miss your inconsistencies and your chaotic nature.
I miss your inappropriateness.
I miss your love even though when you were here
I never knew you loved me.
Daddy, you caused the most pain in my life, and
I still miss you.

Walking in sane
As I walk, I step out of insanity into sanity.
Looking back I could piece together
Some steps along the way that inspired my growth,
Like the time when my father pulled two knives on me.
Shocked, I took two steps back
And realized I was staring into the face of insanity.
I took the high road and left,
Wow, how close I came to becoming a statistic.
Another time was when a friend pulled a gun out
And pointed it directly at me. I looked directly into his eyes
And realized there was no one home.
I fled into another room and waited until sunrise and snuck out
Like a thief in the night.

All along my path I could see how I gained strength and courage
To walk in sanity.

One month later I traveled to Punta Cana, Dominican Republic, just to relax. For the last four years I had been taking care of my father. Now I felt a certain freedom. In December I traveled to Barbados and decided to move there. After living in Barbados for a year, I was invited to move to Washington, DC, and open the Inner Journeys Holistic Healing Center. I decided to combine my gifts, life lessons, and story to use as healing tools and share with others. I teach forgiveness and share my life experiences through lectures, short stories, poetry, and art. I offer my collection of poems, "*Inner Journey, The Walk of a Poet*" as an expression of the challenges of love, universal love, unconditional love and forgiveness.

Forgiveness and healing helped me to evolve into a wisdom keeper and indigenous healer. After three years, I relocated the healing center to Philadelphia.

Author Afterthoughts

I learned I had to forgive in order to heal. Anger and rage are destructive emotions. I began by trying to understand my parents and what made them do what they did to me. How could this happen, and why did this happen? I learned through this process and understanding that my parents were also victims of abuse and abandoned as children; they were simply repeating the patterns they had learned. I was the sacrificial lamb used by my mother to keep my father at bay. She was using the survival skills she learned as a child. Both of my parents were surviving the only way they knew how. When I understood this, it help begin the process of forgiveness and relieve the anger.

Inner Journey, The Walk of a Poet

Contents

Insanity

Break-Up

Universal Love

Foreword

A collection of prayers, observations, and life experiences.

Hope

Perfection

The desperate need for perfection.

Imperfection is intoxicating because it
makes me feel more human.

The more imperfect someone is, the
more unconditional love flows.

It's within the imperfection that you
have an abyss of acceptance.

The Colors of Spring

The colors of spring

Awaken my excitement about the future.

My hopefulness increases.

My laughter becomes louder.

My wishes becomes clearer, when I see the colors of spring.

My creativity awakens.

The colors of spring announce to the
world it time to be reborn.

Blink

With a blink of an eye,

There will be sun.

With a blink of art,
There will be spring.
In the flip of a toe and a look into my eyes,

Summer.

Hollowness

In the hollowness of my soul, there is a cry for justice.

In the hollowness of my soul, there is a cry for love.

In the hollowness of my soul, there is a cry for equality.

In the density of my bones, there is pain, soot, and disrespect.

My heart wants freedom.

My soul demands freedom.

My spirit fights for freedom.

Beautiful

Kissed by the angels.

When you are kissed by the angels,

You know everything is in balance.

Body, mind, and spirit are synchronized.

You walk on your soul's path.

You speak your soul's desire into existence.

Love

A Special Kind of Love

When two soul mates from a past life recognize each other,

This is a special kind of love.

They linger around each other and
absorb love as deep as a well.

They are amused with the sight of each other.

After they share love, they are willing
to share love with others.

Allow the bells of humanity to ring.

The Flavor of Love

Love is a special seasoning.

It cannot be layered.

It must stand on its own.

It often comes as a surprise ingredient.

The punch of flavor caught right at the tail end of an evening.

A surprise pop in your heart.

A flavor that is unfamiliar yet very captivating.

The flavor of love taste different every time.

He Called Her Spiritually

He was hoping she didn't leave before he spoke with her.

His connection to her was very deep.
She was the one person who could knock him off his square.

Her kind of love can only be understood by those who are
willing to take a risk and have courage to open their hearts.

He called her spiritually.

With one glance he called her spiritually
On an inhale of his breath.
She understood the rhythm,

Unspoken gestures, rhythmic movements,
and an insatiable appetite for love.

He called her spiritually.

Twinkle

Can you see the joy and twinkle in his eye
And the thoughtfulness of his gestures?

Can you feel the love that permeates the entire room?

All the moves he makes are making steps toward her love.

He finds comfort in her love.

He reaches and touches the fullness of her lips and remembers how supple they are.

Balance

Love silences rage.
Where there is love, there is peace.

He is balanced by her.
No one understands the higher purpose of this union.
Even though there has been pain, struggle, and lust,

They are bonded.

He knows he can come to her for unconditional love.

She offers a love that is pure,
A love that tastes as sweet as honey,
A love that brings justice to the soul.

Hunger

He looked into her eyes and started feeding on her spirit,
like a tick on a dog.

She looked into his eyes and saw his hunger.

She sensed urgency in his need for her love.

She allowed him to connect to her vital source
and take one cup and one cup only to nourish his soul.

Reaches

He reaches for her.

He reaches for her in her eyes.

He looks to make sure the connection is still there.

He looks, connects, and reaches for her.

With an open heart, begging for her to
return, pouring his heart out,
He reaches into her soul and tries to open her heart again.

With an act of desperation,

He laid his heart out on the table.

He left to return to his responsibilities,

Feeling assured

His heart was now her responsibility.

Restore

He has a love so deep and wide as the sea.

Unfortunately he is not connected to this love, because he is with the other women who represent everything unlike love.

She has a love that will full up his cup.

She has a love that will restore his faith back to life.

She has a love that will restore his belief back in humanity.

Be in Love

Love surrounds her because she allows love in her life.
She allows love in her heart.
She allows love in her aura.
Her intention is to give love, be love, and receive love.
We ask all who have the intention to give love, be
love, and show up to be an example of love.

How do you know love? Do you love casually?
Inner circle love, outer circle love,
Out of your mind, smack your mamma love.
Or is your love reserve, check the computer love?

Love provides justice.

Teaching love is a priority.
We teach every day about love with our walk.
Do you walk in the world full of hope?

As you walk, with love do you feel your heart expand?

With love there is a sense of hope.

He Misses Her

He misses her from the depth of his pores,
from every cell of his DNA.

Every fiber in his body has called for her.

There has been silence in the physical
world, but not in the spiritual world.

There are many things that need to be said,

Another part of the story that needs to be told.

No one can block this love. This love is still growing.

The Lover

The lover will contact her because
He misses her; he loves.
She must not be alarmed by his dysfunctional behavior.
He’s been led by illusions.

When they look in each other’s eyes,
there is a soul connection.
With a soul connection, there is a reminder of love.
Where there is a reminder of love,
their hearts will be uplifted.
When these two come together, there
will always be a place for love.

Spirit Connection

A lot was said without speaking.

Their spirits connected in a dance of rhythm and movement.
They became symbiotic with their
steps, their energy and flow.

Their spirits dance to their own melodies.

Secrets

No one knows their secrets,
Secrets that kept them bonded.
He has followed her from one lifetime to another,
Secrets that are not in this poem.

Secret love.

Touching his aura through his heart,
Every time she sees him, it's like the first time.

Every moment with him is fresh and brand new.
He can't help but follow her from lifetime to lifetime.

Secrets.

His Love

When he is around, I feel beautiful.

I feel connected to light.

I am love when I'm with him.
His love for me has allowed love to
flow from me to the world.

He consistently loves me; I can rely on him
like the sunrise and the sunset.
His love sustains me and propels me into another level.

His love touches me so I may touch the world.

Sending Love

The wind can blow and bring an enormous
abundance of respect and love.

As he sits in another house with someone else,
he sends her enormous amount of love.

He thinks of her.

She cannot hide from him and his love.

Their love is everlasting.

It will always be.

She cannot escape it.

Even under the layers of sadness, tears, and longing,

there sits love.

Temptation

Her scent drives him.

Her scent drives him like a navigation system.

It's intense and puts him on cruise control.

Her scent is like an antenna.

He refuses to acknowledge the power of her love.

When they are apart, it grows stronger and stronger.

As he tries to repair the other relationship,
his thoughts are on her.

Love Transcends

Love transcends borders.
Love transcends state lines.
Love transcends universes.
Love transcends flowers given out of obligation.

It's much more important to have love than a diamond ring.
It's better to have love than to have someone who
doesn't have the capacity to show you love.

We Are

He talks about her like she's a queen.

He talks about her like she is his fantasy.

He has the highest respect for her.

He wants to be in the light around her.

I want to be in your space.

I want to breathe in your air.

I want to walk in your steps.

Wherever you are, I want to be right beside you.

We Are One

I don't know if I can live without him.

I don't know if I can have breath without him.

My air is his air. My breath is his breath.

My lungs are his lungs.

I can see out of his eyes, and he can see out of my eyes.

We are one.

Taste

I want to taste him.

I want to taste the sweat on his brow.

I want to taste him when he enters.

I want to taste him after we made love.

I want to taste him after he tells me he loves me—

The sweet taste of him.

He arouses every one of my senses.

He allows freedom of expression.

He allows all that is beautiful within me to surface.

Barriers

Love has no barriers.
Love is not perfect.
There is no beginning, no end to us.
Our love is like sucking on a peppermint, cool in my mouth.
Our love can also be like a piece of chocolate,

Sweet, smooth, and satisfying.

Touch

He touches my foot; he touches my ankle.
He puts his hand at the smallest part of my leg.
His touch defines me as a woman.

Value

You make my life important.

I live to hear your voice.

My value increases when I spend time with you.

I'm more a woman with you.

My heart expands, and my capacity to love increases.

You give value to me.

Seeing Him

Seeing him is a renewal of my spirit.

Seeing love through his eyes,

Looking deeper, I saw sadness.

Him pleading with God, “Why can’t I be with her?”

His soul begs for freedom.

His soul looks for love.

His soul looks to be recognized.

His soul seeks redemption.

His soul looks out from a dark pit.

His soul thinks of a time when we will be together again.

Insanity

Insanity

You're living on the edge of insanity.

Every now and then you get in bed with insanity.

When you make love to insanity, you wake up crazy.

Insanity will make you think you have nothing.

Insanity will make you think you have no options.

Insanity will make you think the only option
is to get back in bed with insanity.

Insanity will have you making unhealthy choices.

Deny

She denies her truth even when confronted.

She denies herself in the mirror.

She denies and defends her ambassador.

When the authentic self shows up, she denies her.

With Anger

With anger come sadness.

With anger comes disappointment.

With anger comes dysfunction.

With anger comes regret and mistakes.

With anger comes loneliness.

With anger comes the darkening of the soul.

She Hid

She hid behind global talk.
She hid behind a pretty smile.

She hid behind sexual glances.
She hid behind sex.
She hid, which led her into the recesses of her mind,
Alone, dark, and angry.

She hid behind addictions.
She hid behind shopping.
She hid behind chocolate cake.
She hid behind clutter,
And in the middle of clutter, she found chaos.
She wanted a loving relationship but accepted abuse.
She said she wanted fun, but was a professional mourner.

She hid behind mimicking, and no one knew
who she really was, not even her.
She hid behind lies and stories.

She ran from the truth, love, and intimacy,
So she hid.

She Hid and Ran

She hid and ran in the corners of her mind,
Always keeping one foot in front of what
She thought was danger.
She would walk quickly, turn around to
check, and then walk quickly again.

Where was she going?
The destination did not matter,
As long as she had one foot in
Front of the perceived danger.

Dawn turn into sunset, sunset into dawn.
She never respected time.
Time slipped right out of her hand.
One day she looked up and noticed her dark hair
Had turned to gray.

She finally realized all along she had been running away from
Her authentic self.

Hesitation

Hesitation has put cement around your feet.
Hesitation has puts locks around your heart.

Everyone can see you are not available.
Step out of the cement, and let the ropes of insanity go.

Empty Eyes

Looking at empty eyes and seeing there
is no one looking back at me,

Looking deeply,

Looking for the person I once knew.

Looking for the friendship I once had.

Looking for the love but seeing emptiness.

It's Your Choice

You are protected but not connected.

You are protected but lonely.

You are protected but afraid and scared.

You are protected but angry and cold.

It's you choice.

Do you want protection or do you want love?

Do you want to be loved?

Step out from behind your wall and choose love.

Alone

I am alone and lonely.

I am alone, angry, and upset.

I am alone wondering who cares.

I am alone, sad, and depressed.

I am alone, unable to reach inside.

Darkness prevails.

Crazy

Crazy will seek you out.

Crazy was waiting on the corner of your
block, with a smile on her face.

Crazy left blood on your doorbell.

Crazy can be beautiful with curves.

Crazy went to the alley and met you
at the back door creeping.

You woke up, crazy was standing over your bed with a knife.

Crazy broke in while you were sleeping.

You need to put crazy down.

Mimic

I mimic you because I don’t know who I am.

I mimic you because I don’t know how to be myself.

Married to Insanity

Life is going on while insanity is in your heart.

Life is going on while you live your life on pause.

Life is going on while you are in the town in your mind.

Life is going on while you are thumb sucking, and feeling
sorry for yourself, because you are married to insanity.

Lack

I was so connected to lack.
Lack was washing my feet with guilt.
Lack will ask to borrow your car to go on a job interview.
Lack has no boundaries, character, or integrity.
Lack and crazy meet regularly to create a losing game plan.

Pain

I don't want my pain to choose my mate.

I don't want my pain to choose my career.

I don't want my pain to choose my neighborhood.

I have allowed pain to destroy my life.

The Truth

She sat with her false self, telling untruths.

The truth was bigger than her.

The truth swallowed her whole,

And the truth shut her down.

The only person you can change is the person in the mirror.

If looking outside of you, you are living in denial.

Embrace your truth and become one with spirit.

You pretend to be lost and confused.

What is your truth?

Break-Up

Heart

How can you sit in front of me without your heart?

How can you sit in front of me and
pretend we are just friends?

How can you sit in front of me and
talk as though I don't matter?

How can you sit in front of me knowing my heart is for you?

Is it possible somewhere in the silence of your mind?

You can rediscover our love, or has it been lost?

How do you sit in front of me without showing me you care?

Guilt

When you are sitting in the park, and
you are supposed to be working.

Guilt has drained all of your motivation.

When you pull up in front of your home and you
realize you haven't made enough money for the
day, guilt has been your business partner.

When you put your key in the lock, guilt opens the door.

When you look her in the eyes and say I love
you, guilt is looking back at you.

When you hear guilt say, I love you and a piece of
you dies, because you are there out of obligation and
you know guilt has become your spiritual partner.

Guilt can kill you.

Empty Promise

Fear of love attacks all of his senses.

Before entering her home, he can feel the intimacy.

The smell of intimacy washes over him like a pheromone.

It washes over him like a personal summer.

Before he enter her house, his spirit leaves his body.

He doesn't remember what happened.

I Remind Him

I remind him of all he doesn't have.

I remind him of all he missed out on.

I remind him of love.

I remind him of tenderness.

I remind him of respect.

I remind him of softness,

Flowing one to another.

I remind him.

I remind him he still has a heart.

I remind him he deserves to be loved.

He knows where he is right now is so far
away from of what I remind him of,

So he suffers right along with me.

We sit with the loneliness.

Our hearts are yearning for each other.

I Needed You

I needed you.

I needed your taste.

I needed your smell.

I needed your essence.

Where were you?

Were you with her, thinking about me?

Were you with her feeling bound by your obligations?

Were you with her feeling stifled, miserable, and dirty?

When you free yourself from the bondage of her,

You will realize how much of our
precious time you have wasted.

I needed you.

Heartbreak

Even though he has hearts and pink roses, I am not available.

Even though he touched me in places that no one
had ever touched me, I am not available.
Even though my heart cries every night
for him, I am not available.

Even though I feel empty inside without
him, I am not available.

Even though my feet feel like they are in cement
and cannot move, I am not available.

Even though my hearts is broken in pieces and no
one will ever be able to put it back together,

Even though I have been split in half,

I have reached a point of no return.

My love, our love, was combined, and now we have separated.

There are pieces of me that will always
be missing because you left.

Fill Me

You either want to swallow me whole or run away.

There is no middle ground—let's be friends or let's be lovers.

You are not feeling me like I'm feeling
you—you're just feeling my ass.

I need you to feel me in your heart.
I need you to breathe my love and know that I am for real,

Feel my knowledge of our past lives together.

Fill me with your caring; fill me with your unconditional love.

Feel me whole.

Fill me.

Love Blessing

There will come a time when his name

Will be a memory

And no longer be a point of pain.

There will come a time when his name
will put a smile on my face.

Joy and happiness will return.

The will come a time when his name will
bless the entire room with love.

Your Heart Yearns

When love is absent, your heart yearns.

When love is absent, your mind wonders on days gone by,

The sweet memories of fun and laughter.

He remembers the first glance.

He remembers the comfortable feeling of familiarity.

He will never forget the love and the
total acceptance of his heart,

Her heart to his heart,

Wishing upon wishing to see and feel
the glory of sharing again.

Touched to My Core

There is a part of my heart that will always miss him.

There is a part of my heart that he touched
and still waits for him to return.

He held me like his last breath

He kissed me like a succulent piece of candy.

Doubt

She doesn't think I have the capacity to love her.
She doesn't take me serious.
She does not know me.
She does not know my heart.
She does not know my abilities and capabilities.
She has not felt my love.
My love put a period at the end of her sentence.

Universal Love

We Love

We used love as a reason for living.
I reveal light and love to the world.
I am what I am because of you.
We are one.
We are here, and we are now because we are love.

We Work

We work by magic and miracles.
We work by generosity.
We work by unconditional love.

Illumination

Oh the beautiful light, is it the light of the sun?
No, it's the illumination of your soul.
It's the illumination of your spirit.
Bring forth all of your goodness, and
Share it with the world.

Love Sees

The meaning of love sees the brightness of every heart.

Joy.

May your well beings keep you happy.

May your well beings lead you to joy.

Where there is love, there is hopefulness.

Where there is love, there is forgiveness.

Have faith in the unseen, and remember
kindness goes a long way.

One with Spirit

When you are one with spirit, you are balanced.

When you are one with spirit, you are equal.

When you are one with spirit, you are loved.

When you are one with spirit, you walk in faith.

When you are one with spirit, you are connected.

When you are one with spirit, you are humble.
When you are one with spirit, you connect with humanity.

When you are one with spirit, you love freely.

When you are one with spirit, you are.

The Ocean

The ocean is speaking to us.
The ocean wants us to come.
There is healing at the ocean.
There is love at the ocean.
There is forgiveness at the ocean.
There is letting go of regret at the ocean.
Come now, do not hesitate. Let go.
The spirit of the ocean is calling you for this blessing.
Let the ocean bless you.

We Bless

We bless all the inhabitants of the earth.
We bless one by one from the brain to the feet
so there is clarity as you walk your path.
We come to create love.
We bless, and with this blessing, we
bring harmony and peace.

We Come to Assist

We come to assist the inner journey of the soul.

We come to assist the soul to evolve.

We are the old souls here to assist you.

We will be your mentors.

We will be the gatekeepers.

We will be the door openers.

We Are Here

We are here to show the world that there is love.

We are here to show love.

We are here to impart love on the masses.

We are here to heal with love.

We Are the Light

I let go of the old.
I let go of the past.
I let go of everything that no longer serves my highest good.
I let go all of people places and things.
I let go of all attachments.
I am looking for optimum health, wealth, love.
And so it is.

We Learned

We learned that with love, you can move mountains.
The art of love equals support.
We learned that being in alignment,
you can achieve your goals.
We learned that by remaining faithful, consistent,
and steady you can have whatever you want.

Truth

This is about truth, honesty, and life.

Walk your sacred path.

Allow your soul to evolve by

Admitting your truth,
Living your truth,

And standing in your truth.

The Creator

I am one with the creator of all that is.
I am a creative creator.
I am more than my body.
I can create abundance, wealth, and prosperity.
I am financially wealthy.
I am wealthy on all levels.
And so it is.

Appear

We appear to you at night.
We appear to you with words of wisdom.
We come to you to connect.
We come to show love.
We come to give lessons.
We come to teach lessons.

Sacrifices

When sacrifices are made, there must be compromise.
When sacrifices are made, sometimes you don't get your way.
When sacrifices are made, the energy is returned,
and you are exonerated and upheld.
Sacrifices are made as the result of experience,
wisdom, and maturity.

Fed by Love

Our lesson is love.

I was fed by love today.

As I was walking, the sun kissed every part of my body.

The flowers smiled at me.

The wind tickled me.

To Be

To be in life is to give love.
Live life on purpose.
Don't get caught up with the illusions.

Sharing and giving love is why we are here.
You must give love and practice forgiveness.

We Come

We come for the optimum healing.
We come to shoulder the wounded.
We come to tie up loose ends.
We come to make a better path.
We come so we can make a better place for the children,
So there can be rebirth and renewal.
We come to settle old debts.
We come to restore harmony, love, and joy.
We come.

About the Author

Kathy Morris is a natural creative channel who shares her gifts with the world through her poetry, writing and energy work. As a survivor of incest and domestic violence, her experiences gave her a unique perspective while working as one of the first women on the Philadelphia police force. After being hit by a car while on duty, she spent 20 years in various healing modalities. Her transformation of the physical, psychological and spiritual pain motivated her to learn how to teach and heal others to experience unconditional love and follow their soul's purpose as she now walk hers. She published her first book of poetry, Inner Journey the Birth of a Poet in 2008 and collaborated with Stephen Wise-Katreil to create a musical CD under the same title. A chapter of this memoir was included in the anthology, The Journey of Healing, Wisdom from Survivors of Sexual Abuse in 2010.

She founded Inner Journeys in 2000 to provide tools, techniques, and products that enable personal transformation to people of all ages.

For more information contact Innerjourneys@att.net or www.innerjourneys-heals.com.

Printed in the United States
By Bookmasters